DOG FOOD COOKBOOK FOR PICKY EATERS

DR. WESLEY GLASGOW

TABLE OF CONTENTS

INTRODUCTION

In the heart of my childhood, I discovered a profound connection that would shape the course of my life – a connection with man's best friend, a connection that sparked a journey into the world of canine companionship and the incredible power of nourishment.

As a child, I was bestowed with the gift of my first dog, Dan. Dan wasn't just a pet; he was a cherished member of our family, a bundle of fur and loyalty that filled our home with boundless joy. In those early years, my love for Dan knew no bounds, and in my innocent desire to shower him with affection, I inadvertently embarked on a journey that would redefine my understanding of dog nutrition.

I bestowed upon Dan everything my young heart deemed delicious – scraps from our table, treats in abundance, and indulgences beyond measure. Dan, in return, basked in the love and attention, unaware of the silent consequences that would soon befall him.

After a couple of years of blissful ignorance, a haunting reality unfolded. Dan, my once lively and exuberant companion, became a shadow of his former self. His boundless energy diminished, replaced by lethargy. His once shiny coat dulled, and his eyes lost their spark. Something was undeniably wrong.

It was a trip to the veterinarian that unraveled the depth of our oversight. The diagnosis was heart-wrenching – Dan had developed diabetes, a condition exacerbated by his unhealthy eating habits. The vibrant spirit that once defined him was now overshadowed by illness, and it was a pivotal moment that etched itself into the fabric of my being.

Dan's meals underwent a radical transformation, guided by the expert hands of the veterinarian. The power of proper nutrition became evident as Dan's health gradually improved. It was a transformative experience, a revelation that ignited a passion within me – a passion to understand, cultivate, and share the profound impact of nutrition on our canine companions.

Fast forward 25 years, and I stand before you not only as a devoted pet owner but also as a veterinarian and seasoned cook. Dr. Wesley Glasgow is the name etched on my professional accolades, a testament to the journey that began with a dog named Dan and evolved into a lifelong dedication to enhancing the lives of our furry friends.

Why, you might ask, does this journey matter to you?

As you flip through the pages of this cookbook, envision the faces of the dogs you hold dear. Picture their wagging tails, those adoring eyes that mirror unconditional love. Consider the responsibility we bear as stewards of their well-being.

What does it mean to nourish our pets?

The benefits are manifold. Healthy eating for dogs isn't just a matter of sustenance; it's an expression of love and care. It's the key to longevity, vitality, and an enduring companionship that transcends the passage of time.

What happens when we neglect this responsibility?

The consequences are stark and heart-wrenching. Obesity, diabetes, digestive issues – ailments that could be prevented with the right knowledge and choices. Imagine the anguish of witnessing your beloved companion endure preventable suffering.

Why is this cookbook your guiding light?

Within these pages, you'll find not just recipes, but a guide to fostering a healthier, happier bond with your pet. It's a compilation of wisdom gleaned from years of experience, a testament to the profound impact of thoughtful nutrition.

In the journey of life, our dogs are steadfast companions, loyal friends who share our joys and sorrows. As you embark on this culinary adventure, may these recipes be the canvas on which you paint a vibrant tapestry of well-being for your cherished companions.

Welcome to the world of love-infused nutrition. Welcome to the transformation that begins with a simple act of caring – feeding your picky eater with the love they so unquestionably deserve.

Contact the Author

Thank you for reading my book! I would love to hear from you, whether you have feedback, questions, or just want to share your thoughts. Your feedback means a lot to me and helps me improve as a writer.

Please don't hesitate to reach out to me through

glasgowesley@gmail.com

I look forward to connecting with my readers and appreciate your support in this literary journey. Your thoughts and comments are valuable to me.

Chapter 1
Why a Cookbook for Picky Eaters?

As pet owners, we understand the challenges of having a picky eater in the family. Dogs, like humans, have unique taste preferences, and convincing them to eat a balanced and nutritious diet can sometimes feel like a daunting task. This cookbook aims to address the common struggles faced by dog owners with finicky eaters, providing insights into understanding your dog's preferences and offering delicious recipes that will entice even the most discerning canine palates.

The Picky Eater Challenge

We all know that feeling of excitement when we present our furry friends with a new and nutritious meal, only to be met with a turned-up nose and a disdainful look. Picky eating in dogs can be caused by various factors, including health issues, boredom, or a simple dislike for certain ingredients. Whatever the reason may be, it's essential for pet owners to find a solution that ensures their four-legged companions are receiving the nutrients they need to thrive.

Tailoring Meals to Your Dog's Tastes

Every dog is an individual with unique tastes and preferences. Some dogs may love the savory aroma of meat, while others may prefer the crunch of vegetables. Understanding what makes your dog's taste buds tingle is the key to creating meals that they will eagerly devour. This cookbook will guide you through the process of identifying your dog's favorite flavors, allowing you to tailor their meals to suit their specific likes and dislikes.

The Importance of a Balanced Diet

While accommodating your dog's preferences is crucial, it's equally important to ensure they receive a balanced and nutritious diet. This cookbook will provide recipes that not only cater to picky eaters but also prioritize the essential nutrients necessary for your dog's overall health. From protein-packed meals to veggie delights, each recipe is crafted to strike the perfect balance between taste and nutrition.

Building a Stronger Bond

Beyond providing nourishment, mealtime can be an opportunity to strengthen the bond between you and your furry friend. By taking the time to understand their likes and dislikes, and preparing meals that cater to their preferences, you'll create a positive association with food and enhance the joy of shared moments.

Chapter 2

Nutritional Basics for Picky Eaters

Essential Nutrients for Dogs

Understanding the nutritional needs of your picky eater is crucial for ensuring they receive a well-balanced diet. Dogs, like humans, require a combination of essential nutrients to thrive. These include:

1. **Protein:** An essential building block for muscle development, repair, and overall body maintenance.

2. **Fats:** Provide a concentrated source of energy and contribute to healthy skin and coat.

3. **Carbohydrates:** A vital energy source, promoting digestive health and providing dietary fiber.

4. **Vitamins:** Support various bodily functions, including immune system health, vision, and bone development.

5. **Minerals:** Essential for bone health, fluid balance, and overall metabolic processes.

6. **Water:** Fundamental for hydration, nutrient absorption, and temperature regulation.

Tailoring Recipes to Dietary Needs

Creating meals that cater to your dog's dietary preferences requires a thoughtful approach. Consider the following tips:

1. **Protein Sources:** Identify your dog's favorite protein sources. Whether it's lean meats, poultry, fish, or plant-based proteins, incorporating their preferred protein into meals can increase palatability.

2. **Texture Matters:** Some dogs have texture preferences. Experiment with different textures—crunchy, moist, or a mix of both—to discover what your picky eater prefers.

3. **Variety is Key:** Offering a variety of ingredients ensures a diverse nutrient intake. Rotate proteins, vegetables, and grains to keep meals interesting and nutritionally complete.

4. **Homemade Treats:** Integrate homemade treats into your dog's diet. These can be used as rewards during training or as special snacks, adding an extra layer of variety to their meals.

Balancing Homemade Meals

When preparing homemade meals for your picky eater, achieving a balance of nutrients is essential. Keep the following guidelines in mind:

1. **Consult with a Vet:** Before making significant changes to your dog's diet, consult with your veterinarian. They can provide insights into your dog's specific nutritional needs and offer guidance on homemade meals.

2. **Protein-First Approach:** Ensure each meal has a good source of high-quality protein. This could be meat, eggs, or plant-based proteins like lentils or beans.

3. **Incorporate Healthy Fats:** Include healthy fats such as olive oil, fish oil, or flaxseed oil to support skin, coat, and overall well-being.

4. **Watch for Allergies:** Pay attention to your dog's reaction to different ingredients. If allergies or sensitivities are identified, adjust recipes accordingly.

5. **Moderation is Key:** While variety is essential, moderation is equally important. Avoid excessive treats or foods that may be high in salt, sugar, or unhealthy fats.

By paying attention to your picky eater's nutritional needs, tailoring recipes to their preferences, and ensuring a balanced diet, you can create meals that are not only delicious but also contribute to their overall health and happiness. In the following chapters, we'll explore specific recipes designed to cater to various tastes while meeting these nutritional principles.

Chapter 3
Protein-Packed Recipes

Chicken & Sweet Potato Delight

Cooking Time: 30 minutes

Servings: 4 servings

Ingredients:

- 2 boneless, skinless chicken breasts

- 1 cup sweet potatoes, diced

- 1 cup carrots, finely chopped

- 1 tablespoon olive oil

Instructions:

1. Preheat the oven to 375°F (190°C).

2. In a bowl, toss chicken, sweet potatoes, and carrots with olive oil.

3. Spread the mixture on a baking sheet and bake for 25-30 minutes until chicken is cooked through.

4. Cool, then shred the chicken.

5. Serve in portions suitable for your dog's size.

Nutritional Information: Protein: 22g, Fat: 8g, Carbs: 15g

Beef & Quinoa Medley

Cooking Time: 25 minutes

Servings: 6 servings

Ingredients:

- 1 pound lean ground beef

- 1 cup quinoa, rinsed

- 2 cups spinach, chopped

- 1 tablespoon coconut oil

Instructions:

1. Cook quinoa according to package instructions.

2. In a skillet, brown the ground beef in coconut oil.

3. Add spinach to the skillet and cook until wilted.

4. Mix in cooked quinoa and stir until well combined.

5. Allow the mixture to cool before serving.

Nutritional Information: Protein: 18g, Fat: 12g, Carbs: 20g

Salmon & Brown Rice Feast

Cooking Time: 15 minutes (if rice is pre-cooked)

Servings: 5 servings

Ingredients:

- 2 cups cooked brown rice

- 1 can (14 oz) salmon, drained

- 1 cup peas, frozen or fresh

- 1 tablespoon fish oil

Instructions:

1. In a bowl, combine cooked brown rice, flaked salmon, and peas.

2. Drizzle with fish oil and mix until ingredients are evenly distributed.

3. Serve in appropriate portions for your dog.

Nutritional Information: Protein: 20g, Fat: 8g, Carbs: 15g

Turkey & Pumpkin Stew

Cooking Time: 20 minutes

Servings: 4 servings

Ingredients:

- 1 pound ground turkey

- 1 cup pumpkin puree

- 1 cup green beans, chopped

- 1 teaspoon turmeric powder

Instructions:

1. Brown ground turkey in a skillet.

2. Add pumpkin puree, chopped green beans, and turmeric powder.

3. Simmer until green beans are tender.

4. Allow to cool before serving.

Nutritional Information: Protein: 16g, Fat: 10g, Carbs: 12g

Lamb & Lentil Casserole

Cooking Time: 30 minutes

Servings: 5 servings

Ingredients:

- 1 pound ground lamb

- 1 cup lentils, cooked

- 1 cup carrots, diced

- 1 tablespoon olive oil

Instructions:

1. Cook lentils according to package instructions.

2. In a skillet, brown the ground lamb with olive oil.

3. Add cooked lentils and diced carrots, cooking until carrots are tender.

4. Allow the casserole to cool before serving.

Nutritional Information: Protein: 24g, Fat: 14g, Carbs: 18g

Chicken Liver Delight

Cooking Time: 35 minutes

Servings: 3 servings

Ingredients:

- 1 cup chicken livers, trimmed
- 1 cup sweet peas, frozen
- 1/2 cup brown rice, cooked
- 1 tablespoon coconut oil

Instructions:

1. In a pan, sauté chicken livers in coconut oil until fully cooked.
2. Add sweet peas to the pan and cook until heated through.
3. Mix in cooked brown rice and stir until well combined.
4. Allow the dish to cool before serving to your discerning pup.

Nutritional Information: Protein: 19g, Fat: 10g, Carbs: 15g

Tuna & Potato Patties

Cooking Time: 20 minutes

Servings: 5 servings

Ingredients:

- 2 cans (5 oz each) tuna in water, drained

- 2 medium-sized potatoes, boiled and mashed

- 1 egg, beaten

- 1 tablespoon parsley, chopped

Instructions:

1. In a bowl, combine drained tuna, mashed potatoes, beaten egg, and chopped parsley.

2. Form the mixture into patties and cook in a lightly oiled skillet until golden brown on both sides.

3. Cool before serving this delectable tuna and potato delight.

Nutritional Information: Protein: 22g, Fat: 6g, Carbs: 18g

Venison & Carrot Stew

Cooking Time: 40 minutes

Servings: 4 servings

Ingredients:

- 1 pound venison, diced

- 1 cup carrots, sliced

- 1 cup white rice, cooked

- 1 tablespoon olive oil

Instructions:

1. Brown venison in olive oil until fully cooked.

2. Add sliced carrots and cook until tender.

3. Mix in cooked white rice and stir until everything is well blended.

4. Allow the stew to cool before serving this savory delight to your furry friend.

Nutritional Information: Protein: 26g, Fat: 10g, Carbs: 16g

Pork & Pumpkin Mash

Cooking Time: 25 minutes

Servings: 3 servings

Ingredients:

- 1 cup ground pork

- 1 cup pumpkin, cooked and mashed

- 1/2 cup quinoa, cooked

- 1 teaspoon flaxseed oil

Instructions:

1. In a pan, cook ground pork until fully browned.

2. Mix in cooked and mashed pumpkin, then add cooked quinoa.

3. Drizzle with flaxseed oil and stir until thoroughly combined.

4. Allow the mash to cool before serving.

Nutritional Information: Protein: 18g, Fat: 9g, Carbs: 14g

Sardine Surprise

Cooking Time: 15 minutes

Servings: 2 servings

Ingredients:

- 1 can (4 oz) sardines in water, mashed

- 1/2 cup carrots, grated

- 1/2 cup green beans, finely chopped

- 1 tablespoon fish oil

Instructions:

1. Mash sardines in a bowl and add grated carrots and finely chopped green beans.

2. Drizzle with fish oil and mix until well combined.

3. Serve this nutritious and quick sardine surprise in portions suitable for your pup.

Nutritional Information: Protein: 15g, Fat: 8g, Carbs: 12g

Chapter 4
Wholesome Carbohydrate Options

Sweet Potato & Turkey Casserole

Cooking Time: 40 minutes

Servings: 4 servings

Ingredients:

- 2 cups sweet potatoes, peeled and diced

- 1 pound ground turkey

- 1 cup peas, frozen

- 1 tablespoon coconut oil

Instructions:

1. Steam or boil sweet potatoes until tender.

2. In a skillet, brown ground turkey in coconut oil.

3. Mix in steamed sweet potatoes and peas.

4. Allow the casserole to cool before serving to your pup.

Nutritional Information: Protein: 24g, Fat: 12g, Carbs: 20g

Brown Rice & Beef Stew

Cooking Time: 35 minutes

Servings: 5 servings

Ingredients:

- 1 cup brown rice, uncooked
- 1 pound lean beef, diced
- 2 cups carrots, sliced
- 1 tablespoon olive oil

Instructions:

1. Cook brown rice according to package instructions.
2. In a pan, brown diced beef in olive oil.
3. Add sliced carrots and cooked brown rice, mixing well.
4. Allow the stew to cool before serving.

Nutritional Information: Protein: 22g, Fat: 14g, Carbs: 18g

Pumpkin & Chicken Medley

Cooking Time: 30 minutes

Servings: 4 servings

Ingredients:

- 1 cup pumpkin, cooked and mashed

- 2 boneless, skinless chicken breasts, cooked and shredded

- 1 cup green beans, chopped

- 1 teaspoon turmeric powder

Instructions:

1. In a bowl, combine mashed pumpkin, shredded chicken, chopped green beans, and turmeric powder.

2. Mix until ingredients are evenly distributed.

3. Serve this wholesome medley in portions suitable for your dog.

Nutritional Information: Protein: 20g, Fat: 8g, Carbs: 15g

Quinoa & Lamb Pilaf

Cooking Time: 25 minutes

Servings: 3 servings

Ingredients:

- 1 cup quinoa, rinsed

- 1 pound ground lamb

- 1 cup spinach, chopped

- 1 tablespoon coconut oil

Instructions:

1. Cook quinoa according to package instructions.

2. In a skillet, brown ground lamb in coconut oil.

3. Add chopped spinach and cooked quinoa, stirring until well combined.

4. Allow the pilaf to cool before serving.

Nutritional Information: Protein: 18g, Fat: 12g, Carbs: 20g

Oatmeal & Turkey Patties

Cooking Time: 20 minutes

Servings: 4 servings

Ingredients:

- 1 cup old-fashioned oats, cooked

- 1 pound ground turkey

- 1/2 cup carrots, grated

- 1 tablespoon parsley, chopped

Instructions:

1. Cook oats according to package instructions.

2. In a bowl, combine cooked oats, ground turkey, grated carrots, and chopped parsley.

3. Form the mixture into patties and cook until golden brown.

4. Serve these wholesome turkey patties to your picky eater.

Nutritional Information: Protein: 16g, Fat: 10g, Carbs: 12g

Barley & Salmon Delight

Cooking Time: 45 minutes

Servings: 5 servings

Ingredients:

- 1 cup barley, cooked

- 1 can (14 oz) salmon, drained

- 1 cup carrots, diced

- 1 tablespoon fish oil

Instructions:

1. Cook barley according to package instructions.

2. In a bowl, combine cooked barley, flaked salmon, and diced carrots.

3. Drizzle with fish oil and mix until ingredients are evenly distributed.

4. Allow the delight to cool before serving.

Nutritional Information: Protein: 24g, Fat: 8g, Carbs: 15g

Chickpea & Turkey Stew

Cooking Time: 30 minutes

Servings: 4 servings

Ingredients:

- 1 can (15 oz) chickpeas, drained and rinsed

- 1 pound ground turkey

- 1 cup zucchini, diced

- 1 tablespoon olive oil

Instructions:

1. In a pan, sauté ground turkey in olive oil until fully cooked.

2. Add diced zucchini and chickpeas, stirring until zucchini is tender.

3. Allow the stew to cool before serving.

Nutritional Information: Protein: 22g, Fat: 10g, Carbs: 18g

Lentil & Chicken Soup

Cooking Time: 40 minutes

Servings: 6 servings

Ingredients:

- 1 cup lentils, rinsed

- 2 boneless, skinless chicken breasts

- 2 cups sweet potatoes, diced

- 1 tablespoon coconut oil

Instructions:

1. In a pot, combine lentils, chicken breasts, diced sweet potatoes, and enough water to cover.

2. Simmer until lentils and sweet potatoes are tender, and chicken is cooked.

3. Shred the chicken and mix well before serving this comforting soup.

Nutritional Information: Protein: 26g, Fat: 12g, Carbs: 22g

Buckwheat & Pork Stir-Fry

Cooking Time: 25 minutes

Servings: 3 servings

Ingredients:

- 1 cup buckwheat, cooked

- 1 cup ground pork

- 1 cup broccoli florets

- 1 tablespoon soy sauce

Instructions:

1. Cook buckwheat according to package instructions.

2. In a pan, brown ground pork and add broccoli florets.

3. Mix in cooked buckwheat and soy sauce, stirring until well combined.

4. Allow the stir-fry to cool before serving.

Nutritional Information: Protein: 18g, Fat: 10g, Carbs: 15g

Millet & Duck Casserole

Cooking Time: 35 minutes

Servings: 4 servings

Ingredients:

- 1 cup millet, cooked

- 1 pound duck breast, sliced

- 1 cup butternut squash, diced

- 1 tablespoon olive oil

Instructions:

1. Cook millet according to package instructions.

2. In a skillet, sear duck breast in olive oil until fully cooked.

3. Add diced butternut squash and cooked millet, stirring until well combined.

4. Allow the casserole to cool before serving.

Nutritional Information: Protein: 24g, Fat: 14g, Carbs: 18g

Chapter 5
Healthy Fat Additions

Salmon & Coconut Oil Blend

Cooking Time: 15 minutes

Servings: 3 servings

Ingredients:

- 1 can (14 oz) salmon, drained

- 2 tablespoons coconut oil

- 1/2 cup carrots, finely chopped

- 1 tablespoon parsley, chopped

Instructions:

1. Mash drained salmon in a bowl.

2. In a small pan, melt coconut oil over low heat.

3. Add finely chopped carrots to the melted coconut oil and sauté until tender.

4. Mix the mashed salmon, sautéed carrots, and chopped parsley until well combined.

5. Allow it to cool before serving this healthy fat blend to your pup.

Nutritional Information: Protein: 18g, Fat: 12g, Carbs: 8g

Avocado & Turkey Delight

Cooking Time: 20 minutes

Servings: 4 servings

Ingredients:

- 2 ripe avocados, mashed

- 1 pound ground turkey, cooked

- 1 cup blueberries

- 1 tablespoon flaxseed oil

Instructions:

1. Mash avocados in a bowl.

2. In a separate skillet, cook ground turkey until fully browned.

3. Mix the mashed avocados, cooked ground turkey, blueberries, and flaxseed oil until well combined.

4. Allow it to cool before serving this delightful and healthy fat addition.

Nutritional Information: Protein: 22g, Fat: 16g, Carbs: 10g

Sardine & Spinach Mix

Cooking Time: 10 minutes

Servings: 2 servings

Ingredients:

- 1 can (4 oz) sardines in water, mashed

- 1 cup spinach, cooked and chopped

- 1 tablespoon olive oil

- 1/2 cup quinoa, cooked

Instructions:

1. Mash sardines in a bowl.

2. In a pan, heat olive oil and add chopped and cooked spinach.

3. Add the mashed sardines and cooked quinoa to the pan, stirring until well combined.

4. Serve this nutritious and quick sardine and spinach mix.

Nutritional Information: Protein: 15g, Fat: 10g, Carbs: 12g

Peanut Butter & Banana Bliss

Cooking Time: 5 minutes

Servings: 2 servings

Ingredients:

- 1/2 cup natural peanut butter

- 2 ripe bananas, mashed

- 1/4 cup oats, rolled

- 1 tablespoon honey

Instructions:

1. In a bowl, mix natural peanut butter, mashed bananas, rolled oats, and honey.

2. Stir until the ingredients form a smooth and creamy blend.

3. Allow it to cool slightly before serving this blissful and healthy fat addition.

Nutritional Information: Protein: 10g, Fat: 18g, Carbs: 20g

Flaxseed & Chicken Spread

Cooking Time: 15 minutes

Servings: 3 servings

Ingredients:

- 1 cup cooked chicken, shredded

- 2 tablespoons ground flaxseed

- 1/2 cup apples, finely diced

- 1 tablespoon plain Greek yogurt

Instructions:

1. Shred the cooked chicken and place it in a bowl.

2. Add ground flaxseed, finely diced apples, and plain Greek yogurt.

3. Mix until well combined, creating a spreadable consistency.

4. Allow it to cool before serving this tasty and healthy fat spread.

Nutritional Information: Protein: 15g, Fat: 12g, Carbs: 10g

Coconut & Blueberry Infusion

Cooking Time: 10 minutes

Servings: 3 servings

Ingredients:

- 1/2 cup coconut oil, melted

- 1 cup blueberries

- 1/4 cup chia seeds

- 1 tablespoon honey

Instructions:

1. Melt coconut oil in a pan over low heat.

2. Add blueberries, chia seeds, and honey to the melted coconut oil.

3. Stir until the blueberries release their juices and the chia seeds absorb the liquid.

4. Allow it to cool before serving this antioxidant-rich and healthy fat infusion.

Nutritional Information: Protein: 6g, Fat: 22g, Carbs: 15g

Almond & Turkey Medley

Cooking Time: 15 minutes

Servings: 4 servings

Ingredients:

- 1/2 cup almond butter

- 1 pound ground turkey, cooked

- 1 cup pumpkin puree

- 1 tablespoon coconut oil

Instructions:

1. In a bowl, mix almond butter, cooked ground turkey, pumpkin puree, and melted coconut oil.

2. Stir until all ingredients are well combined.

3. Allow it to cool slightly before serving this nutrient-packed and healthy fat medley.

Nutritional Information: Protein: 20g, Fat: 16g, Carbs: 10g

Hemp Seed & Tuna Surprise

Cooking Time: 10 minutes

Servings: 2 servings

Ingredients:

- 1 can (5 oz) tuna in water, drained

- 2 tablespoons hemp seeds

- 1/2 cup green beans, finely chopped

- 1 tablespoon fish oil

Instructions:

1. Mash the drained tuna in a bowl.

2. Add hemp seeds and finely chopped green beans to the mashed tuna.

3. Drizzle with fish oil and mix until well combined.

4. Allow it to cool before serving this surprising and healthy fat addition.

Nutritional Information: Protein: 18g, Fat: 12g, Carbs: 8g

Chia Seed & Beef Blend

Cooking Time: 20 minutes

Servings: 3 servings

Ingredients:

- 1 pound lean beef, cooked and shredded
- 2 tablespoons chia seeds
- 1 cup sweet potatoes, mashed
- 1 tablespoon olive oil

Instructions:

1. Shred the cooked beef and place it in a bowl.
2. Add chia seeds, mashed sweet potatoes, and olive oil.
3. Mix until well combined, creating a savory and healthy fat blend.
4. Allow it to cool before serving.

Nutritional Information: Protein: 24g, Fat: 14g, Carbs: 18g

Sunflower Seed & Turkey Mix

Cooking Time: 15 minutes

Servings: 4 servings

Ingredients:

- 1 cup ground turkey, cooked

- 2 tablespoons sunflower seed butter

- 1/2 cup carrots, grated

- 1 tablespoon plain Greek yogurt

Instructions:

1. Cook the ground turkey until fully browned and place it in a bowl.

2. Add sunflower seed butter, grated carrots, and plain Greek yogurt.

3. Stir until well combined, creating a delightful and healthy fat mix.

4. Allow it to cool before serving.

Nutritional Information: Protein: 18g, Fat: 14g, Carbs: 10g

Chapter 6
Sneaky and Delicious Treats

Pumpkin & Peanut Butter Bites

Cooking Time: 20 minutes

Servings: 15 treats

Ingredients:

- 1 cup canned pumpkin

- 1/2 cup natural peanut butter

- 2 cups whole wheat flour

- 1 teaspoon cinnamon

Instructions:

1. Preheat the oven to 350°F (175°C).

2. In a bowl, mix pumpkin, peanut butter, whole wheat flour, and cinnamon until a dough forms.

3. Roll the dough into small balls and place them on a baking sheet.

4. Flatten each ball with a fork and bake for 15 minutes.

5. Allow the treats to cool before serving these sneaky and delicious bites.

Nutritional Information: Protein: 3g, Fat: 5g, Carbs: 10g

Blueberry & Oat Cookies

Cooking Time: 25 minutes

Servings: 12 cookies

Ingredients:

- 1 cup blueberries, fresh or frozen

- 1/2 cup oats, rolled

- 1/2 cup coconut flour

- 1/4 cup coconut oil, melted

Instructions:

1. Preheat the oven to 325°F (163°C).

2. Mash the blueberries in a bowl.

3. Add rolled oats, coconut flour, and melted coconut oil to the mashed blueberries, mixing until a dough forms.

4. Scoop spoonfuls of the dough onto a baking sheet and flatten each with the back of a spoon.

5. Bake for 20 minutes until golden brown.

6. Cool before serving these sneaky and delicious cookies.

Nutritional Information: Protein: 2g, Fat: 6g, Carbs: 8g

Carrot & Apple Pup cakes

Cooking Time: 30 minutes

Servings: 8 pup cakes

Ingredients:

- 1 cup carrots, shredded

- 1/2 cup apples, finely diced

- 1 cup whole wheat flour

- 1/4 cup honey

- 1/4 cup plain Greek yogurt

Instructions:

1. Preheat the oven to 350°F (175°C).

2. In a bowl, mix shredded carrots, diced apples, whole wheat flour, honey, and Greek yogurt.

3. Spoon the batter into cupcake liners and bake for 25 minutes.

4. Allow pup cakes to cool before serving these sneaky and delicious treats.

Nutritional Information: Protein: 3g, Fat: 2g, Carbs: 15g

Cheese & Bacon Biscuits

Cooking Time: 25 minutes

Servings: 20 biscuits

Ingredients:

- 1 cup cheddar cheese, shredded

- 1/2 cup bacon bits, cooked and crumbled

- 2 cups oat flour

- 1/4 cup water

Instructions:

1. Preheat the oven to 325°F (163°C).

2. In a bowl, combine shredded cheddar cheese, bacon bits, oat flour, and water.

3. Knead the mixture into a dough, then roll it out and cut biscuits with a cookie cutter.

4. Place biscuits on a baking sheet and bake for 20 minutes.

5. Cool before serving these sneaky and delicious treats.

Nutritional Information: Protein: 4g, Fat: 6g, Carbs: 12g

Turkey & Cranberry Jerky

Cooking Time: 3 hours

Servings: Varies

Ingredients:

- 1 pound turkey breast, thinly sliced

- 1/2 cup cranberries, dried

Instructions:

1. Preheat the oven to 200°F (93°C).

2. Arrange turkey slices on a baking sheet and sprinkle dried cranberries on top.

3. Bake for 3 hours until the jerky is dried and chewy.

4. Allow it to cool before serving these sneaky and delicious jerky strips.

Nutritional Information: Protein: 20g, Fat: 1g, Carbs: 5g

Banana & Cinnamon Puffs

Cooking Time: 15 minutes

Servings: 20 puffs

Ingredients:

- 2 ripe bananas, mashed

- 1 cup oat flour

- 1 teaspoon cinnamon

- 1 egg

Instructions:

1. Preheat the oven to 350°F (175°C).

2. In a bowl, mix mashed bananas, oat flour, cinnamon, and beaten egg.

3. Spoon small portions onto a baking sheet and bake for 12 minutes.

4. Cool before serving these sneaky and delicious banana puffs.

Nutritional Information: Protein: 2g, Fat: 2g, Carbs: 10g

Salmon & Sweet Potato Rolls

Cooking Time: 40 minutes

Servings: 12 rolls

Ingredients:

- 1 can (14 oz) salmon, drained

- 1 cup sweet potatoes, cooked and mashed

- 2 cups whole wheat flour

- 1 egg

Instructions:

1. Preheat the oven to 350°F (175°C).

2. Mash drained salmon and mix it with mashed sweet potatoes, whole wheat flour, and beaten egg.

3. Roll out the dough, cut into strips, and roll them into spirals.

4. Place on a baking sheet and bake for 30 minutes.

5. Cool before serving these sneaky and delicious rolls.

Nutritional Information: Protein: 5g, Fat: 3g, Carbs: 10g

Spinach & Chicken Bites

Cooking Time: 25 minutes

Servings: 15 bites

Ingredients:

- 1 cup chicken breast, cooked and shredded

- 1 cup spinach, chopped

- 1 cup brown rice, cooked

- 1/4 cup plain Greek yogurt

Instructions:

1. Preheat the oven to 350°F (175°C).

2. Mix shredded chicken, chopped spinach, cooked brown rice, and Greek yogurt in a bowl.

3. Form small balls and place them on a baking sheet.

4. Bake for 20 minutes.

5. Cool before serving these sneaky and delicious bites.

Nutritional Information: Protein: 5g, Fat: 2g, Carbs: 10g

Apple & Chia Seed Muffins

Cooking Time: 30 minutes

Servings: 10 muffins

Ingredients:

- 2 apples, grated

- 1/2 cup chia seeds

- 2 cups oat flour

- 1/4 cup honey

Instructions:

1. Preheat the oven to 350°F (175°C).

2. Combine grated apples, chia seeds, oat flour, and honey in a bowl.

3. Spoon the batter into muffin cups and bake for 25 minutes.

4. Cool before serving these sneaky and delicious muffins.

Nutritional Information: Protein: 4g, Fat: 5g, Carbs: 15g

Zucchini & Cheese Squares

Cooking Time: 30 minutes

Servings: 16 squares

Ingredients:

- 2 cups zucchini, grated
- 1 cup cheddar cheese, shredded
- 1 cup oat flour
- 2 eggs

Instructions:

1. Preheat the oven to 350°F (175°C).
2. Mix grated zucchini, shredded cheddar cheese, oat flour, and beaten eggs in a bowl.
3. Spread the mixture in a baking dish and bake for 25 minutes.
4. Cut into squares and cool before serving these sneaky and delicious treats.

Nutritional Information: Protein: 6g, Fat: 8g, Carbs: 10g

CONCLUSION

As we come to the closing chapter of this culinary journey tailored for our beloved picky eaters, my heart swells with gratitude and anticipation. The echoes of the past, from my first canine companion Dan to the countless furry friends I've encountered in my veterinary practice, resonate in the very essence of this cookbook.

In every recipe shared, every ingredient carefully selected, and every detail woven into these pages, there is a reflection of the unwavering love we share with our four-legged family members. It is a journey of discovery, of understanding, and ultimately, a testament to the extraordinary bond that exists between humans and their canine counterparts.

As you explore these recipes, envision the tails wagging in anticipation, the eager eyes watching as you prepare a meal crafted with love and intention. Picture the shared moments, the gentle nudges for another bite, and the sheer joy that comes from nourishing your picky eater in a way that transcends the ordinary.

This cookbook is not just a collection of recipes; it's a companion on your quest for providing the best for your furry friends. Your experience, insights, and feedback are invaluable. I encourage you to share your honest thoughts, whether it be the joy of seeing your picky eater relish a new dish or the challenges faced along the way.

Your reviews will not only shape the future editions of this cookbook but will also serve as a beacon for fellow pet parents navigating the intricate world of canine nutrition. Let your words be a source of inspiration, guidance, and camaraderie for those embarking on a similar journey.

In closing, I extend my deepest gratitude for allowing me to be a part of your dog's culinary adventure. May the recipes within these pages continue to fill your home with the aroma of love, and may the bonds forged over shared meals be everlasting.

Remember, each pawprint on our hearts is a testament to the profound impact our pets have on our lives. Cherish every moment, savor every shared meal, and may this cookbook serve as a celebration of the beautiful connection we are privileged to share with our picky eaters.

BONUS 1

Interactive Mealtime Games

Mealtime can be a delightful and engaging experience for your picky eater through the incorporation of interactive games. These activities not only add an element of fun to your dog's dining routine but also stimulate their mental faculties. In this chapter, we'll explore various interactive mealtime games to make your pup excited about their food.

1. Scent-Based Challenges

Introduction: Dogs have an exceptional sense of smell, and incorporating scent-based challenges into their mealtime routine can be both mentally stimulating and rewarding.

Game: Sniff-and-Seek Bowl

1.   **Materials:** Your dog's regular food, a puzzle feeder or a snuffle mat.

2.   **Instructions:**

   - Sprinkle your dog's kibble into the puzzle feeder or hide it within the snuffle mat.

   - Encourage your pup to use their nose to find each piece of kibble.

   - As they engage in this game, not only will they enjoy the challenge, but it will also slow down their eating pace.

2. Food Puzzles

Introduction: Food puzzles are a fantastic way to make mealtime an exciting and intellectually stimulating activity. These puzzles can range from simple designs to more complex ones, depending on your dog's preferences and skill level.

Game: Kong Stuffing Challenge

1. **Materials:** Kong toy, your dog's regular food, and a tasty spread (like peanut butter or yogurt).

2. **Instructions:**

    - Fill the Kong toy with a mixture of your dog's kibble and the tasty spread.

    - Freeze the Kong overnight for an added challenge.

    - Present the Kong to your pup, and watch as they work to extract the delicious contents.

3. Hide-and-Seek Treats

Introduction: Hide-and-seek games tap into your dog's natural instincts and provide mental stimulation. This game can be adapted to mealtime by hiding treats or kibble around your home or in specific containers.

Game: Cupcake Tin Challenge

1. **Materials:** Cupcake tin, tennis balls, and your dog's regular food.

2. **Instructions:**

    - Place a few pieces of kibble in each cup of the cupcake tin.

    - Cover each cup with a tennis ball.

- Encourage your pup to find the hidden treats by nudging the tennis balls aside.

4. Slow Feeder Mats

Introduction: Slow feeder mats are designed to slow down your dog's eating pace, preventing them from gobbling down their food too quickly. These mats can be especially beneficial for picky eaters as they encourage them to explore and savor each bite.

Game: DIY Snuffle Mat

1. **Materials:** Rubber mat or towel, fleece fabric strips, and your dog's regular food.

2. **Instructions:**

   - Cut the fleece fabric into strips and tie them onto the rubber mat or towel.

   - Sprinkle your dog's kibble into the fabric strips, allowing them to use their nose to find and extract the pieces.

5. Puzzle Feeders

Introduction: Puzzle feeders come in various designs and are specifically created to challenge your dog's problem-solving skills while rewarding them with their favorite food.

Game: Rolling Treat Ball

1. **Materials:** Treat-dispensing ball and your dog's regular food.

2. **Instructions:**

    *   Fill the treat ball with your dog's kibble.

    *   As your pup rolls the ball around, it dispenses food, making mealtime a playful and rewarding experience.

6. Obstacle Course Feeding

Introduction: Create a mini-obstacle course to add an extra layer of excitement to your dog's mealtime. This not only engages their mind but also incorporates physical activity.

Game: Tunnel Treat Hunt

1. **Materials:** Child's play tunnel and your dog's regular food.

2. **Instructions:**

    *   Place the play tunnel in a secure area.

    *   Scatter your dog's kibble through the tunnel, encouraging them to explore and retrieve their meal.

BONUS 2
30 DAY MEAL PLAN

Day	Breakfast	Lunch	Dinner	Snacks
1	Peanut Butter & Banana Bliss	Salmon & Sweet Potato Rolls	Pumpkin & Peanut Butter Bites	Blueberry & Oat Cookies
2	Banana & Cinnamon Puffs	Turkey & Cranberry Jerky	Zucchini & Cheese Squares	Carrot & Apple Pup cakes
3	Flaxseed & Chicken Spread	Spinach & Chicken Bites	Cheese & Bacon Biscuits	Interactive Feeding Toy
4	Coconut & Blueberry Infusion	Avocado & Turkey Delight	Salmon & Coconut Oil Blend	Turkey & Cranberry Jerky
5	Salmon & Sweet Potato Rolls	Chia Seed & Beef Blend	Peanut Butter & Banana Bliss	Homemade Broths
6	Blueberry & Oat Cookies	Hemp Seed & Tuna Surprise	Spinach & Chicken Bites	DIY Toppers
7	Turkey & Cranberry Jerky	Pumpkin & Peanut Butter Bites	Apple & Chia Seed Muffins	Food Puzzles

8	Pumpkin & Peanut Butter Bites	Almond & Turkey Medley	Coconut & Blueberry Infusion	Hide-and-Seek Treats
9	Zucchini & Cheese Squares	Chia Seed & Beef Blend	Flaxseed & Chicken Spread	Spinach & Chicken Bites
10	Apple & Chia Seed Muffins	Blueberry & Oat Cookies	Salmon & Coconut Oil Blend	Kong Stuffing Challenge
11	Chia Seed & Beef Blend	Sunflower Seed & Turkey Mix	Avocado & Turkey Delight	Scent-Based Challenges
12	Interactive Feeding Toy	Cheese & Bacon Biscuits	Sardine & Spinach Mix	Turkey & Cranberry Jerky
13	Cheese & Bacon Biscuits	Avocado & Turkey Delight	Peanut Butter & Banana Bliss	Cupcake Tin Challenge
14	Salmon & Coconut Oil Blend	Apple & Chia Seed Muffins	Hemp Seed & Tuna Surprise	Blueberry & Oat Cookies
15	Spinach & Chicken Bites	Scent-Based Challenges	Pumpkin & Peanut Butter Bites	Rolling Treat Ball
16	Carrot & Apple Pupcakes	Pumpkin & Peanut Butter Bites	Zucchini & Cheese Squares	Turkey & Cranberry Jerky

17	Rolling Treat Ball	Blueberry & Oat Cookies	Salmon & Sweet Potato Rolls	Banana & Cinnamon Puffs
18	Sunflower Seed & Turkey Mix	Turkey & Cranberry Jerky	DIY Snuffle Mat	Chia Seed & Beef Blend
19	Hemp Seed & Tuna Surprise	Banana & Cinnamon Puffs	Almond & Turkey Medley	Hide-and-Seek Treats
20	DIY Snuffle Mat	Spinach & Chicken Bites	Blueberry & Oat Cookies	Cheese & Bacon Biscuits
21	Hide-and-Seek Treats	Interactive Feeding Toy	Turkey & Cranberry Jerky	Pumpkin & Peanut Butter Bites
22	Blueberry & Oat Cookies	Coconut & Blueberry Infusion	Sunflower Seed & Turkey Mix	Chia Seed & Beef Blend
23	Kong Stuffing Challenge	Sardine & Spinach Mix	Cheese & Bacon Biscuits	Apple & Chia Seed Muffins
24	Sardine & Spinach Mix	Chia Seed & Beef Blend	Spinach & Chicken Bites	Spinach & Chicken Bites
25	Apple & Chia Seed Muffins	Carrot & Apple Pupcakes	Hemp Seed & Tuna Surprise	Salmon & Sweet Potato Rolls

26	Turkey & Cranberry Jerky	Flaxseed & Chicken Spread	Pumpkin & Peanut Butter Bites	Rolling Treat Ball
27	Blueberry & Oat Cookies	Rolling Treat Ball	DIY Snuffle Mat	Cheese & Bacon Biscuits
28	Coconut & Blueberry Infusion	Pumpkin & Peanut Butter Bites	Chia Seed & Beef Blend	Turkey & Cranberry Jerky
29	Pumpkin & Peanut Butter Bites	Banana & Cinnamon Puffs	Hemp Seed & Tuna Surprise	Scent-Based Challenges
30	Cheese & Bacon Biscuits	DIY Snuffle Mat	Apple & Chia Seed Muffins	Hide-and-Seek Treats

MEAL PLANNER JOURNAL

Meal Planner

Week of:

Monday		Tuesday		Wednesday
BREAKFAST		BREAKFAST		BREAKFAST
LUNCH		LUNCH		LUNCH
DINNER		DINNER		DINNER
SNACK		SNACK		SNACK

Thursday		Friday		Saturday
BREAKFAST		BREAKFAST		BREAKFAST
LUNCH		LUNCH		LUNCH
DINNER		DINNER		DINNER
SNACK		SNACK		SNACK

Sunday	NOTES:
BREAKFAST	
LUNCH	
DINNER	
SNACK	

Meal Planner

Week of:

Monday
BREAKFAST
LUNCH
DINNER
SNACK

Tuesday
BREAKFAST
LUNCH
DINNER
SNACK

Wednesday
BREAKFAST
LUNCH
DINNER
SNACK

Thursday
BREAKFAST
LUNCH
DINNER
SNACK

Friday
BREAKFAST
LUNCH
DINNER
SNACK

Saturday
BREAKFAST
LUNCH
DINNER
SNACK

Sunday
BREAKFAST
LUNCH
DINNER
SNACK

NOTES:

Meal Planner

Week of:

Monday

BREAKFAST

LUNCH

DINNER

SNACK

Tuesday

BREAKFAST

LUNCH

DINNER

SNACK

Wednesday

BREAKFAST

LUNCH

DINNER

SNACK

Thursday

BREAKFAST

LUNCH

DINNER

SNACK

Friday

BREAKFAST

LUNCH

DINNER

SNACK

Saturday

BREAKFAST

LUNCH

DINNER

SNACK

Sunday

BREAKFAST

LUNCH

DINNER

SNACK

NOTES:

Meal Planner

Week of:

<table>
<tr><td>

Monday

BREAKFAST

LUNCH

DINNER

SNACK

</td><td>

Tuesday

BREAKFAST

LUNCH

DINNER

SNACK

</td><td>

Wednesday

BREAKFAST

LUNCH

DINNER

SNACK

</td></tr>
<tr><td>

Thursday

BREAKFAST

LUNCH

DINNER

SNACK

</td><td>

Friday

BREAKFAST

LUNCH

DINNER

SNACK

</td><td>

Saturday

BREAKFAST

LUNCH

DINNER

SNACK

</td></tr>
<tr><td>

Sunday

BREAKFAST

LUNCH

DINNER

SNACK

</td><td>

NOTES:

</td></tr>
</table>

Meal Planner

Week of:

Monday	Tuesday	Wednesday
BREAKFAST	BREAKFAST	BREAKFAST
LUNCH	LUNCH	LUNCH
DINNER	DINNER	DINNER
SNACK	SNACK	SNACK

Thursday	Friday	Saturday
BREAKFAST	BREAKFAST	BREAKFAST
LUNCH	LUNCH	LUNCH
DINNER	DINNER	DINNER
SNACK	SNACK	SNACK

Sunday	NOTES:
BREAKFAST	
LUNCH	
DINNER	
SNACK	

Meal Planner

Week of:

Monday			
BREAKFAST			
LUNCH			
DINNER			
SNACK			

Tuesday			
BREAKFAST			
LUNCH			
DINNER			
SNACK			

Wednesday			
BREAKFAST			
LUNCH			
DINNER			
SNACK			

Thursday			
BREAKFAST			
LUNCH			
DINNER			
SNACK			

Friday			
BREAKFAST			
LUNCH			
DINNER			
SNACK			

Saturday			
BREAKFAST			
LUNCH			
DINNER			
SNACK			

Sunday			
BREAKFAST			
LUNCH			
DINNER			
SNACK			

NOTES:

Meal Planner

Week of:

Monday	Tuesday	Wednesday
BREAKFAST	BREAKFAST	BREAKFAST
LUNCH	LUNCH	LUNCH
DINNER	DINNER	DINNER
SNACK	SNACK	SNACK

Thursday	Friday	Saturday
BREAKFAST	BREAKFAST	BREAKFAST
LUNCH	LUNCH	LUNCH
DINNER	DINNER	DINNER
SNACK	SNACK	SNACK

Sunday	NOTES:
BREAKFAST	
LUNCH	
DINNER	
SNACK	

Meal Planner

Week of:

Monday	Tuesday	Wednesday
BREAKFAST	BREAKFAST	BREAKFAST
LUNCH	LUNCH	LUNCH
DINNER	DINNER	DINNER
SNACK	SNACK	SNACK

Thursday	Friday	Saturday
BREAKFAST	BREAKFAST	BREAKFAST
LUNCH	LUNCH	LUNCH
DINNER	DINNER	DINNER
SNACK	SNACK	SNACK

Sunday	NOTES:
BREAKFAST	
LUNCH	
DINNER	
SNACK	

Meal Planner

Week of:

Monday	Tuesday	Wednesday
BREAKFAST	BREAKFAST	BREAKFAST
LUNCH	LUNCH	LUNCH
DINNER	DINNER	DINNER
SNACK	SNACK	SNACK

Thursday	Friday	Saturday
BREAKFAST	BREAKFAST	BREAKFAST
LUNCH	LUNCH	LUNCH
DINNER	DINNER	DINNER
SNACK	SNACK	SNACK

Sunday	NOTES:
BREAKFAST	
LUNCH	
DINNER	
SNACK	

Meal Planner

Week of:

<table>
<tr><td colspan="2">

Monday

BREAKFAST

LUNCH

DINNER

SNACK

</td><td colspan="2">

Tuesday

BREAKFAST

LUNCH

DINNER

SNACK

</td><td colspan="2">

Wednesday

BREAKFAST

LUNCH

DINNER

SNACK

</td></tr>
<tr><td colspan="2">

Thursday

BREAKFAST

LUNCH

DINNER

SNACK

</td><td colspan="2">

Friday

BREAKFAST

LUNCH

DINNER

SNACK

</td><td colspan="2">

Saturday

BREAKFAST

LUNCH

DINNER

SNACK

</td></tr>
<tr><td colspan="2">

Sunday

BREAKFAST

LUNCH

DINNER

SNACK

</td><td colspan="4">

NOTES:

</td></tr>
</table>

Meal Planner

Month of:

Sun	Mon	Tues	Wed	Thurs	Fri	Sat